C

SAVING OUR PLANET

SAVE THE ANIMALS!

by
Mary Boone

PEBBLE
a capstone imprint

Pebble is published by Capstone,
1710 Roe Crest Drive, North Mankato, Minnesota 56003
www.capstonepub.com

Library of Congress Cataloging-in-Publication Data is available on the Library of Congress website.
ISBN 978-1-9771-2582-8 (library binding)
ISBN 978-1-9771-2596-5 (paperback)
ISBN 978-1-9771-2602-3 (ebook pdf)

Summary:
Introduces early readers to environmentalist concepts including deforestation, animals and their habitats, conservation, and what they can do to help the environment. Features a real-life example of kids who have made a difference.

Editorial Credits
Emily Raij, editor; Brann Garvey, designer; Svetlana Zhurkin, media researcher; Katy LaVigne, production specialist

Image Credits
Dreamstime: Ji Zhou, 11; iStockphoto: SolStock, 28; NOAA: 200th Anniversary Postcards from the Field, 10; Shutterstock: Cory Seamer, 25, Golden Pixels LLC, 26, Hung Chung Chih, 6, Jay Gao, 14, kakteen, 5, Karin Jaehne, 18, lcswart, 7, Levent Konuk, cover, Magalie St-Hilaire Poulin, 24, mhagen Photography, 21, Monkey Business Images, 15, nattanan726, 4, Pixel-Shot, 23, rebvt, 13, Reimar, 29, Wanida_Sri, 17, Wollertz, 9

All internet sites appearing in back matter were available and accurate when this book was sent to press.

Printed and bound in the USA.
PA117

TABLE OF CONTENTS

Words in **bold** are in the glossary.

ANIMALS NEED OUR HELP

Earth is home to lots of living things besides people. There are many different plants and animals. They live anywhere from rainy jungles to dry deserts. Some even live in cold, snowy places.

The things people do affect wildlife all over. Building cities and farms destroys animals' homes. **Pollution** we make gets into our air, ground, and water. It makes animals sick. Animals cannot always help themselves. Caring for the planet is a good way to help them.

ENDANGERED ANIMALS

Some animal **species** are **endangered**. They are in danger of dying out. These animals could become **extinct**. That means they die out completely.

Many species become endangered because their **habitat** changes. Habitats are natural places where wildlife lives. Forests, ponds, and deserts are a few types. Sometimes people hurt animal homes. We pollute lakes and oceans with trash. We cut down trees to build cities.

One of every four species of mammals is endangered. The black howler monkey is one. These monkeys live in South America's **rain forests**. Many trees there are being cut down to build cities or farms. The howler monkeys are losing their homes. If they don't get help, they could die out.

People help free a North Atlantic right whale from fishing nets.

The North Atlantic right whale is also endangered. There are only 400 left in the world. They get caught in fishing nets. They eat garbage in the water. They get hit by boats. These things hurt or kill the whales.

South China tigers once roamed China's forests. Hunters killed many of them. People destroyed their habitats too. Now these tigers are found only in zoos. One has not been found in the wild for 25 years.

Helping animals is a big job. Many people working together can make a difference.

Will Gladstone was in fifth grade when he learned about the blue-footed booby. This bird lives on the Galapagos Islands. It is endangered. Will wanted to help. He sold blue socks to raise money. He and his brother Matthew started the Blue Feet Foundation. They sold 10,000 pairs of socks and raised more than $130,000.

Can you think of ways to help animals? Try looking for old fishing line and kite string. Birds can get tangled in them. Cities along coasts and rivers often hold cleanups. That keeps plastic and other trash out of the water. Could you help?

Do you like drawing? Make posters about endangered animals. Hang them at school. Are you more of a baker? Hold a bake sale. Donate the money to a wildlife group. The World Wildlife Federation (WWF) lets you adopt animals. You don't bring any home. But your money helps keep habitats safe.

HELPING IN YOUR NEIGHBORHOOD

Endangered animals are not the only ones that need help. You can help the animals in your area. What types of wildlife live near you?

Go bird or animal watching in a nearby park. Visit a wildlife area. These provide habitats for mammals, birds, fish, and plants. Park workers can tell you about threats to local wildlife. They can tell you how you can help.

It is easy to invite wildlife into your neighborhood. A small pond can become home to insects and frogs. A birdbath lets birds splash and drink. Be sure to clean your birdbath often. Dirty water can make birds sick.

Birds can't see clear glass. Millions of birds crash into windows and die each year. Place stickers on your windows birds can see. That helps birds stay safe.

Plant **native** flowers and trees in your yard. These plants grow naturally in a place. They give wildlife food. They also give animals places to live. Plants that are not native can take over. They can replace native plants. That can destroy a habitat.

Don't use **chemicals** on your lawn or flowers to kill insects. Birds or other animals that eat those insects can get sick or die. Rain also washes chemicals into lakes and streams. That can hurt the fish and plants there.

People who care about animals know not to **litter**. But not everyone is so thoughtful. Small animals, fish, and birds can get caught in plastic bags. They can get cut on broken glass. Eating trash can make them sick. Piles of garbage can hurt habitats.

Pick up trash you see on the ground. Teach your friends and classmates not to litter.

Don't feed wild animals. They should not rely on people for food. Animals need to hunt so they can live in the wild. Our food is not good for wildlife. These animals should not get used to being around people. Not all people are kind to animals.

When you go on walks in nature, stay on trails. Then you won't step on animals' homes. Leave shells, nests, and logs where they are. Animals may live in or near those.

It is exciting to see wild animals in parks or on nature trails. But don't ever try to catch them. Taking animals from their habitats can hurt them. Take photos instead.

Wild animals are everywhere. They are in the city and the country. You can enjoy wildlife and keep them safe.

Small changes can make a big difference to wildlife. You can help save animals now. What will be your first step?

GLOSSARY

chemical (KE-muh-kuhl)—a substance made by or used in chemistry

endangered (in-DAYN-juhrd)—in danger of dying out

extinct (ik-STINGKT)—no longer living; an extinct species is one that has died out, with no more of its kind

habitat (HAB-uh-tat)—the natural place and conditions in which a plant or animal lives

litter (LIT-ur)—to scatter pieces of paper or other garbage around carelessly

native (NAY-tuhv)—growing or living naturally in a particular place

pollution (puh-LOO-shuhn)—materials that hurt Earth's water, air, and land

rain forest (RAYN FOR-ist)—a thick forest where rain falls almost every day

species (SPEE-sheez)—a group of animals with similar features

READ MORE

Peters, Katy. *Under the Rain Forest Canopy.* Minneapolis: Lerner Publications, 2019.

Whyman, Matt. *Our Planet: The One Place We All Call Home.* New York: HarperCollins Children's Books, 2019.

Williams, Lily. *If Elephants Disappeared.* New York: Roaring Brook Press, 2019.

INTERNET SITES

The Blue Feet Foundation
bluefeetfoundation.com/about-me

San Diego Zoo Kids
kids.sandiegozoo.org/

Wildlife Conservation
www.ducksters.com/animals/wildlife_conservation.php

INDEX